Seablets

The Funny Sayings of Architect
SEAB TUCK III, FAIA

COMPILED BY
KEM HINTON, FAIA

Seablets

The Funny Sayings of Architect SEAB TUCK III, FAIA

SPECIAL THANKS TO:
Keel Hunt, Robert Hicks, Christine Kreyling, Debi Taylor Tate, Sheila Oliver, Marilyn Hinton, T.J. Hinton, Patti Tuck,
Beth Lokey O'Leary, Bill King, Jim Vienneau,
Judy Wright, Elizabeth Papel, Robert Papel, Terry Tretler,
Paula Harris, Mary Roskilly, Chuck Miller, Josh Hughes,
Gary Everton, Joe Hodgson, Scott Parker, Rachel Sutton,
and all the folks at Tuck-Hinton Architecture & Design

Graphic Design by VNO Design

COLORS ON COVER:
University of Tennessee ORANGE
*(with a tiny dash of Auburn University BLUE,
mainly to keep the three Tuck ladies happy)*

Photo credits: Tuck-Hinton Architects

For more information, please contact:
Mascot Books
620 Herndon Parkway, Suite 320
Herndon, VA 20170
info@mascotbooks.com
www.mascotbooks.com

Library of Congress Control Number: 2018914686

CPSIA Code: PRFRE0119A
ISBN-13: 978-1-64307-044-5

Printed in Canada

To Marilyn and Patti
The wonderful wives of two very lucky men

For the past four decades, I have had the great fortune of working with architect and friend Seab Tuck III, FAIA. He was born in Virginia in 1952, attended Auburn University, and came to Nashville in the mid-1970s.

Starting in 1978, we worked together off and on for four years at the large firm of Gresham, Smith & Partners, and in 1984 we decided to open an architectural design studio. The work and history of our firm was documented for our thirtieth anniversary in The Works of Tuck-Hinton Architects: 1984-2015, yet there is one part that was not appropriately chronicled in that book. Seab says the funniest things.

During all these years, Seab has uttered verbal phrases where he has inserted a different word in the passage than the one normally used, resulting in something incorrect yet totally understood and hilarious. "I'm gonna get a gun and choke him," is perhaps the best example.

Seab is not the first to utilize this entertaining capability, defined in the dictionary as a "malapropism." It is perhaps most famously attributed to Samuel Goldwyn, founder of the movie industry powerhouse Metro-Goldwyn-Mayer. This Hollywood mogul was so well-known for his entertaining statements that the term "Goldwynism" would also define this type of verbal alteration. Yet in addition to this type of utterance, Seab would also deliver perplexing or simply humorous comments.

Early in our firm's years, the staff and I would hear Seab blurt one of these phrases and, upon us collectively recognizing the innocent aberration, we would all laugh. And Seab would laugh as hard as any of us, his self-effacing response evidence of his open, admirable character. I recall that one of our interior designers, Paula Harris, first coined the term "Seablets," and for our annual Christmas party gag gifts, she prepared a small booklet filled with these amusing one-liners.

From that point onward, if I heard another one, I would quickly jot it down and slide the note into a large manila envelope. I remembered Rich Hall's amusing 1984 publication entitled

L: Seab Tuck, III R: Kem Hinton, 1998

SNIGLETS: any word that doesn't appear in the dictionary, but should, and I wondered if my growing stack of Seab's quotes would amount to anything. The result of that more than thirty-year endeavor to document the sayings of one of Tennessee's most talented architects is this modest publication.

Seab's contributions as an architect have brought high recognition including Fellow in the American Institute of Architects, Lipscomb University's "Avalon Leadership Award," Sigma Chi International Fraternity's "Significant Sig Award," AIA Tennessee Chapter's "William Strickland Lifetime Achievement Award, " and induction into the prestigious "Circle Guard" of the Country Music Hall of Fame & Museum. It has been my honor to work beside him, and I hope you enjoy these phrases that have made our long business partnership so rewarding...and just plain fun.

I thank Seab, his lovely wife Patti, and his adorable daughters Tricia and Adrianne for their permission to share with others this collection of "Seablets."

– Kem Hinton

Seablets

Like his continuously unpredictable statements, one never knew what

Seab was going to say next. And it never failed to impress me that even though listeners might not completely understand what this gifted and often hilarious communicator said, they almost always knew exactly what he meant. Although many of these quotes possessed a small note to document when each was uttered, these Seablets are presented here in no particular order or priority. Enjoy!

Explaining the simplicity of a task:

"No big deal. It's as easy as falling off a horse."

Complaining about a public meeting:

"Those people talked me to death."

After a strenuous walk in downtown Birmingham:

"I was worn out, just worn long outed."

About a very memorable event:

"I'll never forget this incident, but...I don't know, I can't remember what it was..."

On a challenging client interview:

"I sure am glad it's now."

Advice to a young architect in our studio:

"Don't stop twice at doing that."

During discussion on a design competition:

"Jump in the fire and either float or burn."

After an employee review:

"She was in a real no big deal."

Before a long planning meeting:

**"I can't take them seriously.
They are too mancy yancy."**

On the firm's financial statements:

"We have had overages and underages."

Assertion regarding a marketing situation:

"We've got both of the best worlds."

Observation at a construction site:

"That condensation could cause some water moisture there."

Remark on text clarity of a construction site sign:

"God bless the ABC's."

Knowing of a committee's indecisive nature:

"I knew they would get siffed."

Concerning an unusual city official:

"That guy's a loner. He's alone and last week he also didn't have any friends."

Complaining about inter-office antics:

"We've got to stop doing the horse around."

Warning after reading a news article:

"If they kill her, she'll be really mad."

On the departure of an employee:

"I am absolutely sure he will soon find out what we found out. If he finds it."

Regarding a key official at Lipscomb University:

"Danny is smart and always coopertistic."

Concerning an unpredictable contractor:

"He's just like a bull in a china closet."

Evaluation of a competing architectural office:

"They'll just fold over and bend under when the going gets tough."

Worrying about a potential problem:

"I think it's a bad situation...it needs an a lert."

Determination to deal with a lackluster subcontractor:

"I'm going to get a gun and choke him."

Regarding the lack of quality in office communications:

"That's about the only time we are alone together."

Observation of an assertive instructor:

"She is smart but has a sharp edgy tooth."

Evaluation of an insane situation:

"It was like a snapper crapper."

Commenting on a classroom at Ensworth School:

"The ceiling is too low. Makes the space feel crunchy."

Said during the Girl Scouts' annual fundraiser:
"These cookies are tight as a board."

Noting the probable success of a public presentation:
"Yes, we've got 'em by the barrel."

Pleased with an important meeting:
"We showed them...
like hook, sinker, and line."

Comment on a contemporary house:
"It has good lines and good blinds."

About a funny individual:
"I laughed so hard I split."

Voicing concern over a design strategy:
**"We'll run into a dead road
in that direction."**

During review of an existing structure:

"That floor level was below flush."

Impressed by a new building material:

"It was just damn-namic."

Comment about a business leader:

**"Is his name really Castro?
What does he sound like?"**

Developer's excuse to destroy historic train shed:
"That's pathetic. It's a sadly ass reason."

Watching someone stumble:
"Not good, but it was funniesh."

Request on applying pressure:
**"You need to burnish it really hard,
I mean like to the dirt floor."**

Regarding an unworkable situation:

"It's not all it seems to look to be up to."

When discussing a deadline:

"It's a week from now, or so I do."

Regarding a friend who enjoys hunting:

**"He shoots dead animals
and then stuffs 'em."**

On a spirited and talkative young lady:

"She's very plurpy."

While discussing a wall at a construction site:

"You need to fix it. You need to thin it up."

Explaining a company policy:

**"Yes, we do reviews every year.
Yes, yearish."**

Following a client presentation:

"I am tired of talking today."

About the annoying sound of a mechanical unit:

"All I can hear is the damn quackle."

Explanation at Fin and Pearl restaurant:

**"I didn't know, so I knew
to go over-ordered."**

Concerned with a potentially saturated material:

"They used really spongy bricks."

About an unpleasant aroma:

"It smells just like that old fish looks."

About a famous country music duo:

"He's stellar. And she shines too, but only once."

When referring to a terrazzo installer:

"He's Italian, and his brother's Italian, too."

Feedback on an interior configuration:

"That design is geometrized."

Before a meeting with neighborhood activist:

**"We gotta be careful cause he's
a no good downward thing."**

Criticism of a new restaurant:

"I didn't like it; it was igg."

Explaining a client's deep pockets:

"The cost is no objection."

Lecturing on the need for better training:

"Sorry, but you've got to walk down that trail without blinders."

At Dotson's restaurant in Franklin:

"Order me something chewy or goey."

Answering a phone call:

"Oh, hello there...how are you up to?"

About his own knowledge of current events:

**"I know what's going on; I've got
my ear to the grindstone."**

Voiced support for a design concept:
"The best idea I've had is his."

Explaining a project's potential smooth sailing:
"Things are good; the rails are greased."

Comment on oral hygiene:
**"I really hate the dentist.
And especially that flossing girl."**

At the conclusion of a planning meeting:

"It's just a tackly idea. So please drop it."

Worrying about a builder's lousy work:

"I'm concerned; this thing brings up a flag."

Regarding a slow cabinet maker:

**"They will always be incomplete
and slack lacky."**

Assertion about a performer:

"She made me laugh and jurgle."

Describing an agitated Ken Roberts:

"He was on the rain path."

Observation of a distant historic preservation agency:

"I don't trust that group, 'cause they act just like a toad group."

Assessment of a brutal winter:

"It's so cold, I will be hard frozen."

Giving a heads-up about a new employee:

"Her name is 'this lady's coming in.'"

On a protective device:

**"Why is a fire extinguisher here?
Not for a fire, or is it?"**

Comment after going to a fast-food joint:
"That thing left a bad taste on my mouth."

About an expected, important phone call:
"It was at three o'clock high."

Advice to a project manager:
**"Don't listen to his way cause
he's down and a crummy dog."**

Thinking about a messy situation:

"It's a quirkle."

Responding to an immediate opportunity:

"We have to go while the goings get hot."

While looking up to the sky:

"That cloud formation looks fluffy and full of rain things."

About C'zann, a micro-brewery near our studio:

"Have a beer? Yes, I'll gulp on it."

Describing the history of a downtown development:

"A lot of water has gone under that dam."

Regarding a property line dispute with CXS:

**"I know the railroad folks will
sell them down their tracks."**

On the fairness of a construction defect settlement:

"It's completely balanced, yee and yangst."

Astonished by an enormous structure:

"Wow! It never amazes me."

Comment during visit to a large arena:

**"Where is the nearest exit so
I know my exiting road?"**

Describing the needs of a tenant:

"It's all on one level maximum or two"

Relaying a Christmas story:

"Oh, it was both frankincense and mirth."

Confirming someone's identity:

**"Yeah, he's Joe Reagan. You know,
the President of the brother."**

Noting the absence of employee:

"Is he out all day, or just today?"

Frustrated over a contractor's delays:

"And the hell-of-it is, is, is..."

Concerning the drawings of an intern architect:

**"It's not very good work.
It's very sloppish."**

About performance of new masking tape:

"The problem with it is it sticks too mean."

Remembering advice from a prominent developer:

**"It's like David Emery used to say...
what did he used to say?"**

Commenting on an early meeting:

**"I know it was at seven.
That's why I was late."**

An important self-evaluation statement:

"I need to get my head screwed on tight!"

Describing a new receptionist:

"I think Valerie has a good shoulder on her head."

Subtle compliment to a fellow architect:

"I hear that all the time about left and right brains, but you lost neither."

Observation made during Monday staff meeting:
"We've got a long week today."

Informing citizens at a public meeting:
"I think the continuity needs
to be continuous."

Regarding highways in Tennessee:
"So, why is it that the interstates
are always jammered up?"

Realizing the time required to prepare a master plan:

"It will take splurtz of time."

On an indecisive official:

"He can never decide because he's wishy wishy."

Regarding use brick on a new building:

"We can send a man to the moon, and here we are still stacking dried dirt together."

Statement during monthly planning meeting:

"I wouldn't do it if I were me."

About an illuminated LED billboard:

"I like that big sign. I can always hear it from the road."

Forecasting a tricky contract situation:

"I'll bet that mouse and cat game ends on a really loud-sounding splat."

Comment on bad news:

"I know it's damnidable."

After examining a hardback publication:

**"This book is full of blank pages,
so it may be added to?"**

Regarding a scheduled monthly discussion:

**"For once, I'd like this meeting
to start on a time clock."**

Advice on most direct road to take:
"Go down and over the pike…"

Describing a client's preferences:
**"I think they want that yard
to be in their yard."**

Responding to a sales pitch:
**"You'll have to convince both of us.
Including me."**

Discussion with structural engineer Terry Scholes:

"Are we on tune with one another?"

About receiving check from delinquent client:

"They can't cheat us without not paying us. Or should they?"

On seeing Jupiter through a telescope:

"Wow, I saw that star and didn't know what I saw, but I saw it."

Discussion about the election of new mayor:

"The situation is now up against the wire."

When requesting a strategy session:

"Yes, we need to meet, the three of us, one-on-one."

On the firm's employee manual:

"We only put the information down once so there's smart redundancy."

Mumbling over an important design feature:

"Been there. Done there, too."

During trip to a construction site:

**"Don't go that way.
It's a really long shortcut."**

Making an offer to assist:

**"I'm always around to help but only
if you find me somewhere."**

Determination to receive long-overdue payment:

"I'm going to play a little hard-story."

Said during an urban planning debate:

**"They like to recommend the right thing
when it's wrong."**

About the condition of an old building:

**"The roof was really leaking. I'm serious,
I mean water and damn everything."**

Acknowledging the pressure of a project:
"We are now behind the line."

Recommendation given to a consultant:
"I don't think you can take me more. I'm not me."

Questioned about existence of an agreement:
"No, but we have an understanding... for us, I'll be that contract."

Urging more forceful response to a builder:
"We need to play a harder ball."

Remembering an important comment:
"Now that I know she said those things to me, we can play dead."

On the destruction of a historic house:
"I can't worry over it. If it happens, it won't happen."

Instructions to a general contractor:

"Take that slab and thicken it down."

Yet another critique on a Monday morning:

**"A great movie.
The lady paints and then she dies."**

Attempting to determine a construction schedule:

**"Just like you stick your finger up
in the air to get a number."**

Observing the junk mail sent to our firm:

"You get unindated with those things."

Explanation to a committee meeting:

**"Sorry we are late.
I had a bad clock on my arm."**

When losing patience with an advisor:

**"Rambling about it will only
make you a rambler."**

Request on the treatment of exterior stairs:
"They need to checker those steel plates."

On the potential relocation of an old structure:
**"Whatever is here has nothing to
do with what's there."**

Suggestion before an important presentation:
**"You've got to show like me
and have looseness."**

Investigating a potential job site problem:

"I had to scoop the situation."

Responding to request for design revision:

**"Today, let me look at it
another way tomorrow."**

About an unpleasant beverage late one afternoon:

**"Those taste and smell just like
that place's distilled stuff."**

Discussing the progress of an investment:

"The equity is not up to zero."

Offering an opinion on a new office tower:

**"I don't have to drive by it
every day to see that it's bad."**

Advice to a recent Auburn graduate:

**"You got to walk before you
can crawl around."**

About an owner that cheated his contractor:

"What goes around goes around."

Conveyed during a client presentation:

"Well you know, our reputation doesn't proceed him."

Returning to office after a long code review:

"I can't handle another sour person there. It makes me too sour and gives me sour hives."

Discussing a prominent landscape feature:

"Who, where, and what in that hill?"

After meal in an expensive restaurant:

"The salad was terrible. It was just all that green in one round-ass bowl."

After partner Mary Roskilly asked
if our services were needed:

"I don't know. I have to read their letter to know how."

Expecting the success and failure of a new enterprise:
"What goes up, goes there."

On the driving system in newest Volvos:
"That thing was cool. It drove itself manually automated."

About a picky building inspector:
"She was just way too much of an examinator."

Mentioning the skill of a construction worker:

"He's sure good at operatating that crane."

Recognizing a difficult project budget:

"No matter what, we are now dark frozen."

Hearing that Music City Center will be finished on time:

"Good news! I can finally see the light at the end of the train."

About the design of a Roman aqueduct:

"Those arches were all arching."

Communicating with friend Carter Andrews:

**"We need to go over that,
so just stay in tune."**

Amazed at the beauty of nature in Montana:

**"I was just looking up and then
saw the sky on top."**

About an untrustworthy development company:

"They'll cut you when you turn around."

A philosophical evaluation:

"What happens when my memory leaves my head? Will I know or will you?"

On a discussion with a tardy builder:

"Oh, they'll give you whatever excuse you want."

Stating his availability to resolve a dispute:

"I am handy on an ass-call basis."

At the end of a long partners' meeting:

**"We ought to get more work.
Let's shake the market."**

Comment to another architect in our studio:

**"You have stretched your mind so
far from your mouth."**

Statement in Monday morning staff meeting:

"I wouldn't do it if I were me."

After attending a concert at the Ryman:

**"It's real and that's why
I love bluegrassy music."**

Concern over a barely-operating elevator:

**"I thought it would take both
of us out, but not both."**

On food available at Nashville Farmers Market:
"All those vegetables were fruits to nuts."

Statement after the firm's annual retreat:
"Do people go through weird transgressions?"

Determining number of concert seats to order,
while holding up four fingers:
"No, I need six of 'em."

Decision on an unsatisfactory logo:

"Let's take it and throw it out the drain."

Question posed at Midtown Café:

**"Is this dessert, or is it something
we eat after dinner?"**

Reminding Frist Center's CEO

Chase Rynd of an earlier design concept:

"I know, but it wasn't my idea yesterday."

During a design review:

"I would think, and you would guess."

Recommendation on agreeing with a fire marshal:

"We are going with the tide, but only until the tide comes out."

Comment on liability insurance
with attorney David Garst:

"It's serious if it all boils down."

Upon recognizing a brilliant idea:

"It was just a strike of bolting."

Explaining a design feature to Christine Kreying:

"That design has lots of undulating undulations."

Sudden recognition about a
difficult business decision:

"I don't really care, do I?"

Alerting design team of a sudden idea:
"I have a rough good feeling."

After leaving a city council meeting:
"All I heard was pooh dahs."

On Kerrigan Ironworks 400-foot shed
becoming Riverfront Apartments:
**"It is so long and cool. And with that
smokestack in the distance,
I can just see it zooming cool."**

After passing a statue in downtown Nashville:

"It looked weird and made me crawl."

Demanding clarity in an upcoming presentation:

"We need to be more on spot."

With partner Chuck Miller when evaluating
a schedule for Lipscomb University:

**"Should it be at the end of '02 or '03?
Well, I'll know by the end of the '0' week."**

After hearing sloppy subcontractor's explanation:

"On that excuse, he's pissing up a tree."

Food review during a continuing education seminar:

"I like that sandwich; it's a little dijoney."

Responding to partner

Josh Hughes' lunchtime offer:

**"You're going to walk him through
the building? Why?
Are you going to be there?"**

Reality check on a structural engineering issue:

"That's a little out of my ball game."

Observation about a new residential complex:

"It's a weasey project."

Gary Everton's prank on April 1st, where Seab returned a call to Cumberland Science Museum:

**"May I speak to Sallie Mander?
Yes, I'm sure...Ms. Mander, please.
Well, are there any other Manders?"**

On slow and methodical strategy:

"They need to do that frog in water thing."

Suggesting an approach to renovate a historic prison:

"We need to crawl under the jail."

Regarding feature at an abandoned
industrial complex:

**"I think the smokestack can come
right down. It will probably
really smoke, but that's fine."**

Review of office furniture expenses:

"It cost twice as less."

Concerning an automotive situation:

"It's flat and has no air, too."

On the Andrews family retreat "Wholemeal"
in Beersheba Springs:

**"It has a fire pole in it. Why, because Nelson
wanted one. He discussed and polled his
family on the pole, too."**

Discussing the firm's role in a joint-venture:

"We were going to take a background seat."

Taking a firm stance as a father:

"There's no way I'm going to let Tricia out of a concert at thirteen."

About the driveway to
David Andrews residence:

"There can't be a road up to it. The hill's steep and really tilted."

Justifying an unusual yet beneficial alliance:

"We took that group for advantage."

Following a strenuous meeting:

"I would think that both of us would know, but I'm not sure and now I'm tired."

On an unattractive apartment building and its residents:

"That place is ugly and makes 'em look ugly too."

On an enormous church:

"It's damic huge."

Following a disappointing design presentation:

"Well, I guess we're going to just have to start back at square zero."

Concerned over a group that got swindled:

"They got hooked like a hooker. I mean really hookered."

Bragging about a successful financial maneuver:
"I fakered him off!"

About a protective barrier:
**"Their fencing is really strong, like it's steel
or even a hard metal."**

After joining others in a rendition of
"The Sweetheart of Sigma Chi":
**"It must be the dumbest cool thing
I've ever sung."**

During a retreat in Beersheba Springs:
"I like to sleep long and fast."

After receiving an electrical shock:
**"I got zappered twice by those things.
It still hurts but I try not to think under it."**

On proposed tower above historic
Post Office Building:
**"It should work and just slide down deep
inside and fit like any glove object would."**

Asking an engineer to provide prompt advice:

"We need it quicker than sooner."

During discussion on optional building materials:

"You're making a big mistake and only comparing apples to apples."

Concerning the historic Elm Street Methodist Church (c. 1860):

"There's not enough air in the attic. I may get a coma."

Over a soil scientist's inconclusive report:

"If you don't know, we'll know I won't know."

Comment about staffing decision:

"I don't think anyone can do it but me alone with them."

Predicting the design schedule for
a multi-purpose building:

"It will take two or three good more daily weeks."

Regarding arrest of a prominent individual:
"He's on the hot box."

Deliberating on a design direction:
**"Normally I would be normal,
but this isn't abnormal."**

After Dennis Findley says his
dessert is "warm and beautiful":
"Well, was that pie a woman?"

Evaluation of a wood cabinet detail:

"It looks good, it's a negative reveal."

About confidentiality at the office:

"My files are always locked and yours should look like mine, too."

Describing the headquarters of
Brooks Fiber Communications:

"Those big lines just zipper across the glass walls."

Noting the lack of sheen on a metal handrail:
"That finish is dulled chrome."

Regarding a talk show personality:
**"Rush on AM radio?
Yes, he's rushded-rushed."**

Describing the large garage under
Nashville Public Square:
**"All the parking is below
ground, undergroundly."**

Praise for Leadership Nashville's Jim Blumstein:

"He walks over water."

When offering an opinion to an employee:

"I have a lot to talk to you about but I don't know to talk to you now."

Elevating his alma mater while
noting its pool of rivals:

"All teams in the SEC are great, but Auburn is the best, and the others are pathetic."

Providing advice on a specific building site:
"It's a first-place location."

Delivering a motivational suggestion:
"He should pull himself up with his boots."

Worrying about the presence of too many strong personalities:
"We don't need another chief in the kitchen."

Discussion on amount to charge on an invoice:

"We don't need to be nickley and dimey."

When visiting an existing movie theater:

**"I can feel it doesn't have insulation.
And I can see it, too."**

Excited with the chance to design
a penthouse residence:

**"Incredible location and views from
the tipper toppy floor."**

About a stalled master planning assignment:

"That train is not out of the tunnel."

Discussion on saving an old structure:

**"So it's got a historic façade easement.
Won't they tear up, anyway?"**

On the legacy of a disreputable businessman:

**"I think they'll give him wrath
like hail and brimstone."**

Recommendation to avoid controversy:

"Time for us to just hold quiet."

During a final inspection of a building:

"That ductwork looks just like roundyish metal tubes. Oh, they are?"

When discussing design of the
Country Music Hall of Fame & Museum:

"We're 360 degrees from our original position."

Saddened by the mistake of friend:

"He got rebukered."

Warning during visit of a correctional facility:

**"At that prison,
we might get us cut!"**

Regarding effectiveness of the
office air conditioning system:

**"The mechanical works just fine.
We have plenty of coolness."**

Suggestion on dealing with a new client:

"I'm not sure. We need to feel his water."

After learning about an unfair man:

**"I don't think he'll ever go to heaven.
His wife is too far below."**

About the new Nashville Predators team:

**"I just can't understand hockey.
And I understand almost
everything else, usually, too."**

On an insignificant issue:
"It's that dah lah thing."

On the arrival of daylight saving time:
**"I hate it because I have to
jump up forward."**

Justifying a building code requirement in Brentwood:
**"Of course they require sprinklers.
It takes all the heat and fire
off the fire people."**

Review of a failed marketing presentation:

"It was just blown up to hell."

Regarding an electrical installation:

**"I can know it. The transformer
is transforming just fine."**

After discussion with Dr. Randy Lowry,
president of Lipscomb University:

**"I needed to have a good face-to-face
conversation on the phone."**

Providing a medical evaluation:

"I was sick. My spleen was confused."

Unable to recall his earlier opinion:

**"Somewhere out there you'll
find my thought."**

On the thoroughness of an exceptional
construction company:

**"They are on top of it...
every crook and cranny."**

While watching a hearse in a funeral procession:
"I don't think I'll do that."

Analysis of exterior light fixtures:
"Whatever we do, three's gonna be bigger than four."

Explaining driving procedures
at a very confusing intersection:
"Why do I yield? Do you? No one else does 'cause it ought to be a non-yield road."

Upon making a profitable deal:
"That's just a pocket in my change."

Regarding the use of Kalwall:
**"It's translucent and you also
can't see through it, too."**

Discussion with wife Patti at a
vacation house in Seaside:
P.T. "Why is this railing so low?"
S.T. "Cause it doesn't need to be high."

Alerting others about a nearby resident:

"He's right around the door."

Frank question during an employee's review:

**"What causes you to lose
your temperature?"**

When discussing a dispute between
owner and contractor:

**"Is there something we can do
to make it worst?"**

Request to confirm a code requirement:

"I think we need to validify."

Attempting to keep options open:

**"We aren't burning that bridge,
but it's on fire."**

Right after visit from firm's medical
insurance provider:

**"With all this virus going around,
we have to have in-flu-ence!"**

Impressed with commitment of a consultant:

"He went in with both shoes."

On a local weather forecast:

"Find out about it. I need to know if it's going to rain or just storm."

Comment made right after a holiday open house:

"Her green dress was nice but it was sprayed on too tightly."

Regarding work force labor shortage:

"Anyone who's working has a job."

After returning from a trip to his alma mater:

**"I had to roll down the window
to smell the sounds of Auburn."**

After touring historic Carnton and
its Civil War cemetery:

**"I need to be aware of how old it is and how
long ago other things weren't there, too."**

Commenting on an unfair procedure:

"It's a waste of time, a witch game."

Requesting the attendance of a smart assistant:

**"Ask her to go with me 'cause
I need a wing girl."**

Confirming the dimension of a lab space:

"I know, it's half-way or twice"

On the performance of another's vehicle:

"Your car holds coldness."

Explaining the use of a sketching material:

"I tell them it's trash paper but I really mean it's thiny and trashy."

Regarding his participation at

AIA Tennessee convention:

"I'll do a half-day of that continuing education stuff and a half-day of not."

Impressed with the enthusiasm of a consultant:

"She is a chitty chatty Barbie."

Being informed on a project's progress:

"Seeing as how you think you know, just rev me up to a full speed."

After a lively, positive phone conversation
with a new client:

"That project sounds like a cream de la cream."

Responding about incomplete construction:

"I see what you get."

Upon seeing deer on a hike near Monteagle:

"Yell over and see how they react. I know they'll run and show weakly bones."

Recalling an individual at Leadership
Middle Tennessee fundraiser:

"There's this male guy I met who was so impressive."

Challenge to a talented graphic designer:
"Don't throw out some free-ass logo…"

After looking at the crawl space of Elm Street Church:
**"Under that floor is a thing
just below down under."**

On speaking at public meeting on
Franklin Street Corridor:
**"It's one thing to say that,
and it's another to speak it."**

On a voicemail message to Phil Bredesen:

"So what did I say? I need to know."

Evaluation of a dilemma at Public Square:

**"The problem is that
I don't know the problem."**

Explaining theme of Adventure Science
Center to Ralph Schulz:

**"We wanted to symbolize and reinterpret
the Pyramids and Stone Hedge."**

While pondering his personal responsibilities:
"What is I? How do I?"

About the Richland Creek Apartment complex:
"The ups and downs always give me an ups and downs stomach."

Requesting the right to be forthcoming and honest:
"Let me think through that so when I have a solution, I won't be afraid to give my opinion. And speak my mind out loud."

Before a trip to Europe in the fall of 2009:

"St. Francis of Assisi...is that in Florence?"

Explaining the need for items added to windows:

"Those bug screens keep out all insects except the small, sneaky ones."

Regarding speaking in public:

"I usually get nervous, but then I remember that former boss and then I can never remember anything."

Noting the delay of a project:

"That rolling stone gets moss."

Advice on being diversified:

"You've got to not keep all your eggs in one house."

After discovery of an unknown condition at Lipscomb's Burton Building:

"I can't see it and a camera is not me either."

Self-analysis after a public presentation:

"I'm in oblivion."

Regarding an important presentation:

"They want us to present the interior finishes, but I don't yet see those finishes."

Reconsidering the arrangement of

a presentation drawing:

"This elevation is on top of the other highest elevation."

About a caving adventure long ago:

"We were separately lost in the same place."

Talking about automotive accidents:

"I've only had one wreck that I'd call a wreck."

Reminding others about a company executive's schedule:

"He has an afternoon meeting starting in the morning."

Opinion of a large firm's outings:
"I don't like those company-ass picnics."

Warning of a critical design schedule:
**"We cannot miss that deadline.
It will be dead and we'll die, too."**

Noting location of Warner Bros. Records
executive, Jim Ed Norman:
**"He moved to Hawaii but is
still in Nashville."**

On the anticipated progress by an engineer:
"She'll get her teeth around it."

Asking a friend to be more objective:
**"You wear your feelings
on your shoulders."**

After the author complained about the design
of a small downtown park:
**"Right now, the director is really steamed...
so you need to hang down low."**

Promising to do a winter task for his wife:
"I'll do it right after she's frozen."

Returning from a construction site:
"That wall and its color and insides gave me the biggest hack ache."

On reviewing the balance sheet
of a subcontractor:
"Regarding those finances, they need to have a hands-off feeling."

Pledge to a church building committee:

"We can start on the ground running."

On an upper-level nook at 1810 Hayes Street:

**"It's a cool little space but I could
let her get lost in it."**

Frustrated with a large building committee:

**"I don't know if they'll ever decide.
Right now it keeps on going
back and forth, ping pongy."**

Opinion of a local fundraising event:

"It was a wingy dingy event.."

Advice about a steep concrete road:

**"I can drive down the hill only
if you put your brakes up."**

Complaining about wintertime problems:

**"You would think they have a cure for it,
but my colds are snuffy dark
and can't be fixed."**

After losing federal courthouse design competition:

"We got snarfed."

During a trip in terrible winter weather:

K.H. "If it's ice, your car won't stop."
S.T. "Yes it will. I can make an ice stop."

After a boring presentation by
a window company's representative:

**"I just got tired of it.
It was so ticky ticky."**

Warning about an angry individual:

"He is out for warish land!"

On hiring a new architect from a distant city:

"When she comes over, she'll be over and we'll be out."

Discussing the long relationship with Lipscomb University:

"We've had a lot of water over the dam with you folks."

117

On the space thriller *Arrival:*

"It's a sciency fictiony type of movie."

Distracted by a nearby argument:

**"Cackle is all I can hear, and
I can't take it more."**

On the success of the Country Music
Hall of Fame and Museum:

**"It's run so well because they've got it down
to a tooth-sharp comb..."**

Letting one of the employees take a breather:
"You don't have to be unfocused anymore."

About the firm's manpower during monthly meeting:
"I'm confused. On our long-range schedule, are those short people?"

Wanting to make sure that a contractor and his subcontractors are performing:
"So they're not twiddling their inside fingers."

Wanting publicity in a national design magazine:

"We need you to get into their headlights."

On the impact of Nashville's booming economy:

"It's shocking, and those prices go right out of the roof."

On a historic Art Deco structure

in downtown Nashville:

"It's a cool old building. Slick, curvy, and metally."

Confirming the dimension of a lab space:

"For carbon footprint, use their shoes?"

After visiting a new urban park:

"I'm totally sure. That maple tree was backwards."

After a long meeting on the contents of The Plan of Nashville:

"I hit the wall, and then just felt down all dead and died."

Describing a very famous house in Franklin:

"It's an old, 1925 Antebellum home."

Regarding frequent pranks by a builder:

**"He's a clown and does that
clown funny thing too."**

Regarding the exterior feature above the
Country Music Hall of Fame:

**"We have 78, LP, 45, and CD circles.
That circle will never be unbroken."**

On the code restrictions in a special city district:
"The sign police are down our necks."

Prior to meeting with a company's board of directors:
**"We need to try to do a great
tell and show."**

Confessing a distain for idle discussions
before a fundraiser:
"I don't like all that chitty chattery."

Describing the shape of a corner room:

"It's a squarish circle."

Needing to know the dimensions of a garage:

**"I should know what size it is.
Large or only just big?"**

On the strategy to secure a project by hiring
the client's favorite consultant:

**"We should hire her and be defensive
so she doesn't go elsewhere."**

Explaining a large bruise on his left arm:

"I tripped and fell on a steel iron chair."

Boasting about a probable success:

**"It will be a miracle if we
don't get that job!"**

On the large Mandrell house,

christened "Fontanel":

**"I like those larch logs, but Barbara and Ken
might get tired of all the woodiness."**

Noting the adjacency of a future commission:

"That project is in our back door."

At an interview with a new banking organization:

"We knew we needed to learn Revit, so we just went full cold-turkey into it!"

Looking at options for the floor plan
of The Southern restaurant:

**"Okay, that's the first two.
Now, thirdly and fourthly?"**

During a critique of renderings for a new building:

"On that image, you need to over-gray it."

Noting a pharmaceutical situation:

"They're out of pills. So they need to go get the medification."

Knowing of the firm's need to advance younger staff members:

"We need to release principalship, so we can release project managementship."

About the progress of a new restaurant:

"It should move forward like the wind."

Informing client of his location:

"Okay, I'm on my way.
I'll get there by a momentarily."

Comment on a building to house several
non-profit organizations:

"It's got to be built, or it will
never be built."

Recommendation to move on:

"Give it up. It's just water around that dam."

Describing a successful building dedication:

**"The fun of it is now. Its fun will
last only tomorrow."**

On selection of Paul Stumb as Cumberland University's
new president:

**"That's a good thing to happen.
You can't beat that with a stick."**

Expressing his lack of confidence in a designer:

"I don't care how registered he is."

A few weeks after the death of an influential architect:

"What's Michael Graves going to do, now that he's dead?"

Cautious with a large company's marketing team:

"How can we know that they're not a fake, you know, like a fake-like fake?"

130

Comment on text printed on a large box:

"What does that flat thing say?"

Disposing of old file boxes at Richards & Richards:

"I wish all of my life could fit in these six boxes, because I could sure fill up one."

On the way to see a mock-up for Adelicia condominiums:

"I'll drive fast, so don't let it force you down."

About the office's aging fax machine:

"Well, it just becomes less useless."

On the new phone system:

"When will they make that ignorant, voicy operator operate?"

About the need to decrease the cost
of the Music City Center:

"No lie, we've got to get it in budget and find out all the bass atchet cuts."

Warning about the site for a new house:

"It's too mountainy."

Before yearly meeting with liability insurance agent:

"Tell Don we always want his best price, despite what we or he says."

Urging staff to maintain confidentiality
about Bob Dylan's new distillery:

"Need to be careful...we don't want things to leak and sneaker out."

Admitting to being exhausted after a difficult meeting:

"I'm on half steam."

Giving an excuse to an engineer:

**"I can't think about it now...
my brain is on shut down."**

When reviewing a manuscript:

"I've got to read it to look at it."

Noticing the sound of his new motorcycle:

"It's giving off a sharp noise."

About a retirement home near Crossville:

"Fairfield Glade is great for my parents. But I can't know the glade."

On Marvin Runyon's house near Monteagle:

"His place, 'Skyhigh,' was so special. He loved it and I think he skyed it down every chance."

About a client's legal counsel:

"That attorney is too attornyish."

On his new black Volvo sedan:

"How it goes? I know it goes, really before we start."

Overheard during his phone conversation with close friend:

"Well, Louie, I thought it would be okay to be okay."

Regarding an underperforming carpenter:

"We can't teach that new dog a trick."

On the indecisiveness of a house client:

**"I can't tell what he wants.
He's goosey loosey."**

About item given to staff
members on their special day:

**"You know, if everyone gets a
birthday card, it's never special..."**

Impressed with a contractor's interview:

"He knocked me off my face."

On subtle approach for a marketing proposal:

**"We did that, instead of playing
with the big stick..."**

Discussion on local government's
procedural priorities:

**"They don't get it, and they're putting
the horse before the cart."**

Suggestion on a project marketing strategy:

"They need to bite it off at the pass."

Noting his own personal integrity:

**"I don't really have a vice.
I just have lots of bad habits."**

Observation about the completion
of a difficult master plan:

**"We won't finish the project
until June-ish."**

Boasting about great seats at a concert:

"I was right behind the front."

About his 1970 four-cylinder Honda motorcycle:

**"I must keep it. It still flies,
even with me around it."**

After dealing with a mean waitress in

an inexpensive restaurant:

**"Her face was like a bad
rear-ended trunk."**

Determination to develop an appropriate scheme:

"For the old reasons I'm going to invent."

Commentary on a friend's personal activities:

"No problems with his social life; he can hang out with single married couples."

Discussion with a contractor over knowledge of heavy equipment:

"Have I driven a bulldozer? No, but I'm more dozier than you are."

Quiet lament after an employee's departure:

"Sometimes life is life."

On the treatment of a politician:

**"Boy, they always used to
have his neck on a platter."**

During a round-table discussion with
a management consultant:

**"You need to know that our firm
is niche-ified."**

Questioning the texture of expensive wallcovering:
"Isn't rice paper too crispy?"

Regarding a past presidential election:
"I am so confused. What was that hanging chad doing hanging?"

Determining best way to charge
for design services:
"Okay, we should just go with sour-hourly."

After visiting an old manufacturing facility:

"That stair pops down to a lower level."

Concerning a unique type of structure:

**"What's a yurt? Ha, I know.
It's where they make yu-gurt."**

On accepting a commission to
design a medical facility:

**"We don't normally do this;
it's out of our deal."**

Recognition of one of his best ideas:
"A little bell went off on my head."

Regarding complaints from a political group:
**"Okay, so what do you really
want them to sound?"**

While driving past one of the city's
fast food restaurants:
**"I love annually to get three
White Krystals twice a year."**

Assuring a client about his design experience:
"I had a lot on this. But not a lot."

Regarding issues across the world:
"If they'd just get legal,
they wouldn't need to be legal."

Observation about comment from
recently elected official:
"If I was in his position, I would
probably not say the same thing."

After walking into a new auditorium:

"Imagine we are right now..."

Discussion on travel arrangements:

"Where do you need to fly? I have tickets, but they may not be to that city."

Expressing his opinion of an

expensive Persian carpet:

"It costs a lot, but I don't like it... it's too much ruggy."

Forecasting his health:
"I feel a cold, dankly wind coming on."

Strongly-voiced political comment:
**"I don't like that candidate because
she's just in the left lerch."**

About the constant rivalry between two
Southeastern Conference teams:
**"We don't think Alabama is a state.
It just holds Auburn, and that's enough."**

Evaluation of an unattractive person:

"Gosh, what a bad case of the uglies."

While running late to a meeting:

"I'll drive fast, so don't let that hack you up."

On the spaces in a new building
at Lipscomb University:

"On those walls, you've got to decide if they are walls or not walls."

Concerning an important medical situation:

"It should be a surgeous decision."

Reviewing a design decision for CMA Theater:

**"About that issue, my feeling
is the same as ours."**

Boasting on the successes of his
numerous code variance requests:

**"I never lose an appeal.
I appeal to their appeals."**

Requesting additional information on an investor:

"We must scoop him out."

After purchase of new drafting computers:

**"All we do is spend, spend, spend.
It's like you spend and then you can't."**

While looking at displays in
MBA's Ingram Science Building:

**"What is a symbiosis anyway?
Is it part cymbal or bosis?"**

After reviewing a construction agreement:

"It is a locked-down, iron-tight deal."

About Nashville developer Ray Hensler:

"He's the one who we knew from nobody."

Following discussion on the
purchase of new computers:

**"On that decision, it's now
a cleaner open book."**

Regarding the role of an acoustical engineer:
"He needs to lead the ship."

When interviewing a new intern architect:
"So you're from there?
I guess you grew up there?

On the owner of the Chapple Building,
location of the firm's first office:
"She was a good landlord, but all her restrictions were restrictive."

Describing the employment of a young person:
"Yes, but only for namby part-time."

About a large steel beam:
"That thing is so heavy, but I'm hoping for a downward thing."

Upon hearing about the success
of a new office building:
"They're excited? Good! Tell them that we wanted to knock them down."

During a long design review:

"My point was? Was what?"

An unrealistic yet direct prediction:

"Tomorrow morning he is losing sixty-five pounds."

Pleased with the financial success
of a fraternity brother:

"Hey, with that extra money, he could buy a house in Venice or in Italy!"

Description of Rainbow Falls trail to Mount LeConte:

"It's a real blue funk type of forest."

Culinary recommendation at Fin & Pearl restaurant:

"That's that oil and vinegar stuff you dip bread in."

Describing major tributary that

runs through Nashville:

"The Cumberland River is too watery."

Recalling firm's outing to see *Ferris Bueller's Day Off*:

"All I remember is that I forgot the story."

Attempting to prioritize a design issue first:

"That's a fire requirement and I'm not going to worry about a fire thing now."

Describing grand stair inside
Ezell Center at Lipscomb University:

"You get that vooot, vooot effect."

Comment to bank client Ron Samuels:

"We need to slant that wall over."

During the review of a large auditorium:

"Our height is too low."

Before an alumni meeting of Leadership Nashville:

**"My mind had already told me who
I was going to meet."**

Alerting design team of a sudden idea:

"I need to let the cat out of the box."

After leaving a city council meeting:

"That lady is at my wit's end."

Validating an earlier comment to
mentor Nelson Andrews:

"I just threw that out of the air."

Knowing of the reaction to latest cost estimate:

"I fear the project is dead as a doormat."

On paper clips at the office:

"I hate these things. They always get tangled into a long wire disease."

On Marvin Runyon's leadership
as U.S. Postmaster General:

"I knew he would shake ass!"

Explaining the simple process to obtain a passport:

"It doesn't take a brain scientist."

Determining what days to be away from the office:

"During the holidays, I can't get into this off-schedule."

After a heated budget discussion
with a specialized consultant:

"They're jigging us on the price."

Warning about an unscrupulous lady:

"She was a sheep in fox clothing."

Complaining about insufficient design time:

"I was just halfway in the middle of midstream."

Explaining a requirement in the program for a new structure:

"It needs to have a soft loading dock."

Sudden recognition of a better design option:

"I had a ray of sense."

During an architectural tour:

"Up here on the left, look for that Fay Jones house. But, you can't see it."

While riding in a rented bus on a company trip to Birmingham:

"Remind me before I remember it…"

Concerning an aggressive salesperson:

"Get that dog off my back."

Regarding a famous Tennessee whiskey:

"The green Jack Daniel's is the same as the black one, only green?"

Noting the judge's decision on
a disreputable individual:

"He blown that one out of the court."

Agreeing to do another design review:
"I'll take a fresh look on it."

Deciding to delegate important issue:
**"It's your decision.
It's now in your pocket."**

Wanting a subcontractor to make
his commitment clear:
"We need them to walk the line day one."

Confirming a building's foundation:

"Not a problem 'cause it's on dirt rock."

Describing his friend Rod Maddox:

**"He bikes and bikes and bikes.
He's a biker thing for sure."**

Explanation of Butler's Run renovation on
Historic Second Avenue:

"It was a diamond in the raw."

Voicing satisfaction after attending lecture:

"It was literally literal."

Complaining about slow food delivery:

"I'm starving. When can we expect to smell their answer?"

Knowing of the futility of trying to forecast
a project's final cost:

"You just need to let the chips roll."

On trying to do too much at the Frist Center:

"I painted myself into that box."

Regarding the departure of a disgruntled employee:

"When he leaves, I hope that door really bites him."

Awaiting a decision by Kyle Young, CEO of the Country Music Hall of Fame & Museum:

"It's in his ball cart."

Impressed with Nashville's Fourth of July fireworks:

"That sound was so hard."

Passing the assignment to others in the firm:

**"That's now yours responsibility.
It's into your two courts."**

Question the firm's participation

in a design competition:

"What is we as a firm going to do?"

Upon hearing a service person's excuse:

"I think that is whorse-shees."

After dinner with an out-of-town consultant:

**"Met with him at seven o'clock
on a dammit damn night."**

Discussing the idea of renovating
Nashville's main post office:

"I was thinking out cold."

Questioning the dimension shown on his drawing:

"Well, am I wrong or was I wrong?"

On a session with Cumberland Region Tomorrow:

**"That committee gathering?
I don't know them, do I?"**

Regarding some individuals for their

quick support of a candidate:

"They were in a hurry to jump on the boat!"

Making a new deadline on a delayed project:

"We need to kick it forward."

When asked to participate in a tournament:

"I don't play golf. All you do is run after that little ball."

Complimenting Jerry Williams,

executive director of Leadership Nashville:

"She is smart and quiet-spoken."

Regarding comedian Killer Beaz at Zanie's nightclub:

"He was so funny and also made you laugh."

On recalling his time at Gresham, Smith & Partners:

"Looking back, I wanted to think about them both ways."

Noting the similarities of two sports
during a summer picnic:

"Four square is like short tennis."

Finding an unusual ornament during demolition:

"It was there standing on the wall."

About the Music City Center:

"It's so much larger than I ever dreamed of, and I dream large."

Failing to remember a person's name at annual AIA Tennessee convention:

"I don't have a long memory."

Suggestion during a trip to a local hardware store:

"Don't turn left. That's a death ending."

When discussing gift suggestions:

"What type of things do I need? Ask both of my daughters. One first."

Agreement with an owner to decrease
the size of a building:

"I'll smallen that up."

Explaining his upbringing in Roanoke:

"That's where I lived and, later, grew up."

On firm's continuing education luncheons:

"I hate those classes. All we do is eat and then I have to go learn and know."

Confirmation of the deteriorated
insides of an older structure:

"We both looked at it with my own eyes!"

Compliment on the finish of a new floor:

"It felt smooth as a whistle."

Recalling someone's holiday party:

**"They had way too much to drink
and all got splashtered."**

During discussion at the

Nashville Civic Design Center:

"I really like the stretchiness of that street."

On wasted space in a new facility:

"This is terrible waste. It's all going to God."

Discussion on a contractor's latest estimate:

"Regarding those prices, we need to get that down to reason."

Regarding annual dues to participate
in a local organization:

"For $50 a year, it doesn't cost anything."

Recommendation on trying to generate new clients:
"Let's turn some down stones up."

Evaluating a new engineering firm:
"Do we ever want to work with these guys before?"

Goal for the interior of the Woolworths on Fifth restaurant:
"That needs to be stellular!"

Confirming financial strength of a new company:

"I need some assurity on it."

Concerning the design of the firm's holiday card:

"Why are you so interested in that thing? It only wastes my time schedule."

Concerning effort to obtain a very

important civic commission:

"This project is right down our league."

A different approach to a management dilemma:
"On the other angle..."

Recommendation for an interior arrangement:
"Provide a smaller space, so they can have a two on two discussion."

Noting a developer's treatment
of a fellow architect:
"He ripped him off and blind."

Suggested inclusion of a phrase in AIA Contracts:
"It's for pounding downism."

Hoping that a young individual improves:
"We need that person to be better than that silly crapel."

Regarding a new, very inexpensive residential neighborhood:
"All they are is ticky-tacky houses."

When looking at floor tiles for a new office building:
"Nope. Don't like it. It's too housey."

While in dark area of an abandoned structure:
"Whoa! I have a bad sense of claustrophobia."

After leaving the architecture building
at University of Cincinnati:
"The forms run into each other and co-lide."

183

Facing the arrival of bad weather:

"It's time to buckle down the hatches."

When a large drawing fell off the wall:

**"It dropped down and hit the floor
so hard I choked out."**

After a very strenuous hike into
and out of Savage Gulf:

"You thought I fell off into the earth."

184

Discussing the progress of construction:

"Hand me a shovel so he can go to work."

Concern about a building permit:

"I didn't get an official version, but I know it's official, or you hope so."

Providing a scientific description
of the arrival of nighttime:

"Yes, that's when the sun goes off."

When making a teaming pledge:

"It's all for one, and one for us."

While at AIA National Convention in San Francisco:

"I can't walk another minute. That hour is way too far and my feet have died."

Comment on the height of
Lipscomb University's Allen Arena:

"It's twice as tall as half of ours."

Relaxing with a cold drink after a long meeting:

"I have had a full, empty day."

Confirming his knowledge of this area:

"I know my way all around and all over, and everywhere locally, too."

Wishing that an unruly group of misfits would leave the area:

"They need to take a damn, flying hike!"

Wanting to satisfy a request from Jack Turner:

"We need to get in his eyeballs."

Hearing about a disgruntled code official:

**"She was really mad, and
she chewed him a big one."**

After a long planning session at
Leadership Middle Tennessee:

"The problem was I was there."

Questioning the motivation of a council member:

"I can't quite put your fingers around it."

Regarding a musical instrument:

"I'm sure it was here and sounded very funny. So where is that xyliophone?"

Concern over decision to buy an expensive electrical device:

"It was a hard balance."

After hearing of the impending Great Recession:

"It forces us not to hire-up."

Comment about an object in a very garish house:

**"It had an awful, sparkly,
brassy plastic chandelier."**

Instructions to a Cumberland Region
Tomorrow member:

"You decide. It's either this-ises or thats."

190

On a group's conflicting agendas:

"They will need to march to the drummer."

Providing the location of a reference book:

**"It's right above my desk.
No, my desk desk."**

During a management meeting
at Sole Mio restaurant:

"Those vegetables were just soup to nuts."

191

Confirming advantage of a laboratory consultant:

"We need a sciencey person."

On the selection of several consultants:

"I would give them both Charles, Larry, and Mark."

After meeting with a prominent governmental official:

"I didn't trust him; he seems sketchy."

On the national economy after 2009:

"It was an upturn after a bad turn."

While on vacation at the beach:

"All that sand makes me really all gooey and gritty."

During discussion of design for
Tom Morales' newest restaurant:

"That wall, it needs more roundiness."

Explaining why a governmental advisor was fired:

"He stepped on some wrong toes."

On the annoying habit of a subcontractor:

"Drives me nuts. He makes that spiffy sound all the time."

Noting the steel structure of
Allen Arena at Lipscomb University:

"That upper X-bracing is all X'ed."

Discussing a lost item:

"I'll find it. I almost never do."

On his research of Tuck ancestors:

**"Doing my family history is fun,
but it's always too old."**

Comment about major addition to
Country Music Hall of Fame:

"The floors need to all line up differently."

Knowing that a new project was not confirmed:

"There are too many things in movement."

Acknowledging his forgetfulness:

"I can never remember her name.
All I see is hair and lips."

Regarding the potential success of
a candidate in an important election:

"They say she doesn't have a shot in hell."

Concerning a ruin in England:

"It was made in the Stoner Age."

Responding to new owner about a design fee:

"Where did you get my quote? Even though it says I said that, did I say that?"

Recommending a slight delay in

the delivery of documents:

"Let's do it once the dots are crossed."

Describing the local weather forecast:

"When it's raining, it's only raining."

After visiting a factory:

"Why are you writing that down? Do I need you to remember it?"

Complaining about unfair criticism:

"He still has that guy breathing down his throat."

Comment on a young construction manager:

"He's green behind the ears."

On getting lost in Grundy County:

**"I think we really screwed up.
And screwed to the top."**

Determination to obtain a private school commission:

**"We need to win. We need to do
a harder court press."**

Finding the location of a time capsule:
"It's just there, there."

Annoyed by a consultant's constant movement:
**"He makes all that fidgeting...
always fidgety fidgeting."**

Observation made after a disappointing meal:
**"I think if I was a waiter, and a guy,
I'd find another place to work."**

Dealing with a plumbing engineer:

"I can make some gut feelings..."

Questioning his memory of a client's requests:

"Please tell me now, cause I'm not sure about knowing about what I don't know."

About a meeting of international economic leaders:

"If they think a new world order is good, we need them to order something else."

Noting a person's lack of sobriety:

"He was completely sheddy yastered."

Concerning pursuit of a unique commission:

**"I can run after it, but do
I need to catch it?"**

Informing developer of rising construction costs:

**"The mechanical system price
is out to the sky."**

After receiving a design award:

"We don't want to be all braggy about it."

Being satisfied with the treatment of an interior wall:

**"That is perfect color.
It's a really dark black."**

Discussing the various options in a master plan:

**"We can beat our heads into the ground,
or change and do it a different way."**

Upon reaching the office one morning:

"Sorry I'm late. My tire died."

Confirming his automotive skills:

**"When I drive, I know where
I'm going to get eventually."**

During a discussion on adding new employees:

**"We need to go ahead and order
these people."**

Opinion of an underperforming electrical engineer:
"He's the dumbest person I've ever seen."

About the sons of the late Bob Mathews:
**"Bert and Walker are just like their dad,
only completely different."**

About a thorough residential contractor:
**"Salem was so Salem.
So my place is a Salem, too."**

During tour of an abandoned house:

"It smells really dank."

After interview with a building committee:

**"I don't feel good about that one.
It's probably just a shot in the night."**

Over his treatment of an introductory letter:

**"Why does it always have to be spelled
right? I sure know what he means."**

Said during a scheduling discussion:

"First day of the week? Is that a Monday?"

Confirming the value of a new museum in Music City:

**"It needs to be done in yours
and ours times."**

About moving a large piece of furniture:

**"It takes two people to not
barely pick it up."**

Comment on the minutia of a building code appeal:
"I didn't like that pokey hokey stuff."

On the exterior of a new structure:
"Hard to get away from the glassiness of that building."

Preparing for an important design presentation:
"There are three charms we can use, and I'll use both."

Concerning an overly-vocal committee member:
"He's a sassy ass."

Acknowledging the impact of new technology:
"I get too many useless, important messages on my internet."

Giving an evaluation of project's resolution:
"Everyone is gonna lose out. It's gonna be a zero gain sum."

Joking about his integrity:

"I'm as honest as I'll ever not be."

During a meeting with a traffic consultant:

**"How wide is that road?
I mean, is it wider or just wide?"**

Knowing of his occasional rough language:

**"I'll try not to cuss, but that damn group
knows they're damned too."**

Recommending changes in a marketing effort:

"We need to shuffle the game."

Statement on a large planning assignment:

"On that issue, I need to first get their heads around this."

Concerning his literary absorption:

"When I read, I go slow and only see one page at a time."

Observation of someone with little motivation:

"He's a slack lacker."

Hating to take prescription drugs:

"Medicine is so dumb. You want it to fix you, but you don't fix it yourself."

Receiving his BMW motorcycle insurance policy:

"It was expensive, but it's good all across America including Canada and Alaska."

About a lost briefcase:

"On that one, he took mine with me."

On a local meat-and-three restaurant:

"Remind me before we leave as I always try to know after I order food."

When someone was late to a presentation:

"Did she have directions or not directions?"

Describing black cone feature at the Small residence:

"It's not outside. I mean it's enclosed."

Reflecting on his upbringing:

**"Where I grew up was Virginia.
It seems like that was only then."**

On the name of a new company:

**"Rhythm, movement... I like it
because it's a verb."**

Comment just after a significant weather event:

"When it rains, it storms."

On the firm's previous location:

**"I miss 1810 Hayes Street.
It was a great place for us to be real."**

Discussing appropriate paint color:

**"Yes, you gotta know. It's that reddish shade
of blue. Like purple."**

Noting a bargain on purchase of office furniture:
"They'll buy it. It's a foregone decision."

Heartwarming comment about our office cat:
**"It's not the end of the world.
If she dies, will it be a dead deal?"**

During discussion on appropriate consultants to hire:
**"You convince them. And, then
we take the table off them."**

Advice to an owner on escalating costs:

"Just sit square where you are."

Complaining about relentless requests:

**"They should quit bugging me.
I'm bugged to the earth."**

Noting the end of future downtown apartments:

**"Right now in Nashville, that type
of project is a dead game."**

After meeting with the firm's CPA, Ronny Greer:
"I don't want to beat that financial horse."

While driving in the beautiful Smoky Mountains:
"Don't go down that way.
That road is dead."

Amazed at the success of a new start-up company:
"They get all entrenched, and then
they get their feet in the ground."

Confused over a challenging political situation:

"It's going to dig our head in the sand."

On the interior wall of a new branch bank:

"Stop. That wood pattern is panely paneled enough."

Dealing with nagging backyard problem:

"To get the moles, I will first take two easy steps..."

Describing an unfavorable geotechnical report:

"It's a mess. It's a junk hole…"

About a stalled bill in the federal government:

"Congress will delay and again just hit the can down the road."

When speaking to a prospective employee:

"I like the weather here, especially summer, except July."

Warning about a messy political situation:

"You got yourself into a tar baby."

Rambling about through a dilapidated warehouse:

**"Well, try everything under
that dark light."**

During team discussion on Avenue Bank:

**"It takes a long time to move forward
without it being, like, a long drag."**

Requesting more information about a new client:

"Nobody say anything about anything?"

Sudden observation about a holiday personality:

"Santa has it best. He fools all of us except the dumb elves."

About the return to Internal Revenue Service:

"Move along. They want to get to that tax start thing now and miss any jail bait."

Comment on a disappointing new building:

"You can't see the beauty for the crap."

Comment on new appliance in his house:

**"That ice machine is cool,
but the ice is melty."**

About the character of a library addition:

**"Instead of being like the existing building,
it needs to be all smoothy."**

Critique of the top edge of a metal warehouse:
"The ridge on that roof was too ridgety."

When researching a large parcel of land:
**"You go look for the plats.
It should be in the plater room."**

Reference to design professor at Auburn University:
**"He's like the architect Bruce Goff.
He's a Goffian."**

Advice to a landscape architect:

"It's the value of not being uncertain."

On receiving a traffic ticket:

"What a hassle. I am stuck, like on a soft glue, to it."

On an antique truck he purchased:

"That thing is so fun, with its tough puff motor."

On the participation of new board members:

"You can pick it up or not let them go."

Regarding Tennessee's low unemployment rate:

"We have such a strong workforce that can't get any strength to move."

Awaiting the delivery of new science equipment:

"Will we be safe to say it's there now or should we say it's not?"

Compliment to an interior designer:

"Well, you're young for your age."

About a sensitive political situation:

"We want to make sure to not upset the basketcart."

Warning about a potential jobsite issue:

"Sounds just like something that smells really bad."

Frustrated over the layout of a new school:

"Nothing I know will fit into that box."

On the fast movement of a large truck:

**"That was a bing-slider.
It just slided by me."**

After meeting with an out-of-town contractor:

**"How can we trust that idiot?
Isn't he smart?"**

Making sure that everyone understands a situation:

"The writing is on the table."

During a refueling of his van:

"It's expensive, but that octane has all the right amount of gas in it."

Request to one of the staff members:

"Please find it for me now or before last week goes by."

On the founder and owner of Corsair Distillery:

"Darek is a classy, suity-and-vesty guy."

About the renovation of famous Loveless Cafe:

"It's a restaurant, and now that it's open, you can eat there."

On changing times and his life expectancy:

"Things moving too fast. I'm gonna be dead before she knows it."

After a successful building dedication:

"I'm glad I'm here."

At the end of a construction phrase:

"See that window? It's doing a good job as a hole in that wall."

On a milkshake:

"It had a fruithy flavor and looked quiet good."

Before walking into a negotiating meeting:

"We need to show cooperatism."

Message to receptionist:

**"Find me tomorrow as,
I'm around all today."**

Comment on a floor tile:

**"I don't like it because it's got
that sandy-papery surface."**

Comment made just after lunch on a Friday:

"I've had a wild week today."

Giving advice to a young driver:

"Just apply those brakes without going above the closed alley."

Discussion with a road grading subcontractor:

"Make that hill behave and make it sloppier to the down part."

On the treatment of a conference table:

"It has a course, raspy edge to it."

When scheduling a meeting:

**"Don't you have a new conflict
with that last month?"**

On the aggressive actions of a land planning firm:

**"They should back off or back down.
It's backwards and no one will back it."**

Describing a rooftop garden:

"That's a weird grassy area."

Comment about a tourist couple in Florida:

"They both need to lose weight. Both are weighed out."

Expressing his genuine determination:

"I can stand fast and hard with the best of them. Just listen."

Pondering an important decision:

"I need to think about this. If I was us…"

Request on a road trip to take a different path:

"I'm tired of always going on that super old flippy highway."

Comment on a dumb and cruel woman:

"She can't understand almost anything, and she's a Frankenstein, too."

Describing a new criminal justice facility:

"It's a jail and a courtyard."

Assuring a trusting client:

**"Beyond that horizon,
I'm okay with your cart."**

Trying to build enthusiasm for a new project:

**"You'll need to start and stop twice
at least several times."**

On a respected woman artist:

"She's too funny. She's a talkie walkie."

Request made to lighting consultant Susan Brady:

**"We want as much light as possible.
Like a blaster of light. You got one?"**

On the arrangement of spaces in new office building:

**"The floor plan doesn't work. Even I could
get lost in there, unless I want to."**

During the design review of an important museum:
"That curve is too sharp and offish."

Complaining about a dress code:
**"I hate to wear suits.
I hate to have to be all suitzy."**

On the transformation of Acme Feed and Seed:
**"It's now a restaurant with rooftop bar,
and also even serves food."**

Upon wrapping up a long meeting:
"She sent me into a sloppy trance."

On trying to win an important design commission:
**"Heat 'em up like that hot frog
and water thing."**

When discussing a marketing approach:
**"I can always walk backwards from it if you
think I am walking for it too much."**

Frustrated over a slow-moving project:

"They need to bite that dog in the ass."

Response to an out-of-state consultant:

**"Send me the bill, and I'll think on it.
I have much on my skull right now."**

Pledging to solve problems in a construction contract:

**"It was a huge mess, and she and me don't
know, but think we'll do it on paper."**

After a disappointing meeting with city officials:

"They slammied the door to us."

Remembering a stern but fair mentor:

"I miss his snappy-down talk."

Question about Savage Gulf on
the Cumberland Plateau:

"Is that a canyon or a really deep ditch?"

Urging an electrician to finish his work:

"He needs to put all his teeth to it."

Concern over the selection of a hardware item:

"Why use that soft metalized thing?"

On the activities of a wild lady:

"It's sad. They say all she does is twister around."

Advice to a community planning group:
"You folks must chew that thing up."

Wanting to inspire a design team:
"We can't have any negative negativity."

Remembering a strange event in college:
"I was weirdered out."

While relaxing at the firm's weekly Beer-30:
"Since it's empty, just fill it to the bottom."

After reviewing a design contract:
"His approach was so bass-ackward."

Responding to a critique of his design idea:
"What, too tall? I'll give you too tall!"

On the need to work with a newly-appointed official:

"If you can't beat 'em, beat it."

Providing a suggestion about harsh criticism:

"People in glass houses shouldn't throw."

Concerning a project superintendent:

**"All he does is meander around,
like a meanderall."**

Noting a hazard at new branch bank:

"It's not finished, so watch that slick gravel."

While driving after dark:

"We caught that deer in the floodlights."

On special compote sauce in a unique sandwich:

**"Burger for me! Forget that
compotey-toney stuff."**

Attempting to rationalize his opinion:

"I think high, then think lower."

On phone, describing a project to a builder:

"It's complicated and probably very expensive removal addition."

Discussion on obtaining new projects:

"We need more work? Okay, I'll go get some. I'll be right back."

Reaction to promising design concept:

"That idea, it took me aside."

Selecting a desert at expensive restaurant:

"I want, you know, that baked, like, Alaska thing."

Predicting the outcome of a Metro Council bill:

"Same thing as before, and they'll vote on it again like last year when it all went before and out of style."

Evaluating feature on rendering of a new school:

**"Ditch the pond. It'll be a hassle,
attracting ducks and mallards."**

Explaining his retirement strategy:

**"I'll still be part of the project.
I just don't want to be involved."**

Regarding transition of the firm's ownership:

**"I'm sorry, but Mary, Chuck, and Josh know
best. You and I are now deep toast."**

And this last one was said during a well-attended dedication of the new Daviess County Public Library in Owensboro, Kentucky. When Seab made the following comment about the recognition of the nearby Ohio River in the design of the library, everyone in the crowd nodded in approval, as if they fully understood the comment:

"Symbolism is always important in our projects, and in the children's area, you'll notice the Ohio, interpreted there as a winding waterway pattern on the floor. We wanted to eulogize the river."

Seab's more notable projects:

Music City Center

Country Music Hall of Fame & Museum

Frist Art Museum

Nashville Public Square

Sue & Marvin Runyon Residence

Lipscomb University Allen Bell Tower

Cover of Tuck-Hinton's 2014 book on its first thirty years

For more information, contact:

Kem Hinton, FAIA
5933 Asberry Court, Nashville, TN 37221
(615) 305-1201

Tuck and Hinton